BE HEALTHY

Spirit Says...

BE HEALTHY

A COLLECTION *of* ORIGINAL QUOTES *and* AFFIRMATIONS *to* GUIDE YOU TOWARD OPTIMAL HEALTH

DR. SUSAN BOVA

MARTIN AVENUE PRESS

Copyright © 2016 Susan Bova

All rights reserved. No part of this publication may be reproduced, distributed, or transmitted in any form or by any means, including photocopying, recording, digital scanning, or other electronic or mechanical methods, without the prior written permission of the publisher, except in the case of brief quotations embodied in critical reviews and certain other noncommercial uses permitted by copyright law.

Published 2016
ISBN: 978-1-945262-02-9
Library of Congress Control Number: 2016910939

Book design by Stacey Aaronson

Published by:
Martin Avenue Press
For inquiries, please address:
publisher@martinavenuepress.com

Printed in the United States of America

This book is not intended to be used to diagnose or treat any medical condition, nor should it be used as a substitute for advice from a qualified medical professional. The author offers this only as general information to support you in your healing journey. The author and publisher assume no responsibility for any action taken as a result of using any information in this book.

*To all who have journeyed toward and
all who have achieved optimal health ...
your resolve is the proof that
ALL IS WELL.*

And so it continues ...

A Note from the Author

The road to optimal health is unique to each person traveling it. While the differences are many, there is commonality in every journey – the desire to feel better.

As guidance and wisdom continue to flow from the higher realms, I offer these original quotes and affirmations as support in your healing journey.

Each uplifting passage contains a sub-message of positive reinforcement. Choose a quote, discover that message, then recite the accompanying affirmation for additional support.

It is my wish that, through these words, you find the strength and healing power within you to make the changes necessary to bring you to optimal health.

Spirit says...

- as you move past being stuck during your healing process, you are never alone
- commit to living each moment – NOW
- trust that all is well!

Enjoy a daily dose of uplift, repeat as needed, and may you always welcome optimal health.

With Smiles,
Susan

P.S. At the end of an affirmation, consider adding "And So It Is", "Thank You!", "Yes!", or "Amen" for an extra dose of positive juju.

Spirit Says...

BE HEALTHY

The first step to *healing* is to be willing to *release* the need to harbor physical and emotional ailments. Be willing to *understand* how these ailments have served you, so that through your understanding, you can *release* the need to hold on to them.

Blessings AND POSITIVE ENERGY ABOUND.
THROUGH ANY HARDSHIP,
CHALLENGE,
OR ELATION,
YOU HAVE THE *strength*
TO CONTINUE ON
THE PATH OF YOUR
SOUL'S HIGHEST GOOD.
BE IN *peace* AND
BE WILLING TO *receive*
BLESSINGS AND ENERGY,
SO YOU MAY PASS
IT ALONG TO THE
NEXT SOUL IN NEED.

affirmation

I welcome
positive energy.
I am strong
and I
pass blessings
along.

PHYSICAL FEELINGS OF UNREST ARE TEMPORARY READJUSTMENTS OF THE HUMAN BODY WHILE PREPARING THE SOUL FOR *spiritual advancement.* DURING THESE TIMES, BE MINDFUL NOT TO "OWN" AN ILLNESS. HOLDING ON INVITES THE ILLNESS TO TAKE UP LONG-TERM RESIDENCE, WHICH THEN BECOMES AN EXCUSE FOR NOT ADVANCING SPIRITUALLY. *Let go* AND KNOW THAT *all is well.*

affirmation

My body
temporarily
houses my soul.
I clear
the way for
it to grow.

One way to overcome an addiction to misery is to give yourself permission to *be happy*. May your day be blessed with a *smile* ... let one come to you and give one away.

affirmation

Happiness is a choice. I choose to be happy now.

Do you BELIEVE in the mind-body connection? You think about wiggling your toes and then they wiggle. You desire a smaller mid-section, then you suck in your gut. You're sure you'll be sick, then you start to sneeze. What's not to BELIEVE?

affirmation

My mind and
body work in
perfect harmony.
I manifest
goodness
in my life.

A PRESCRIPTION FOR HEALTH: DON'T WAIT FOR A FRIGHTENING DIAGNOSIS TO *start improving* YOUR HEALTH.  *Start being* HEALTHY TODAY AND LIVE PAST  YOUR PRESCRIBED EXPIRATION DATE.

affirmation

I prescribe my
perfect health
and I
start today.

Has society missed the mark when its biggest curiosity is the results of medical tests? Don't plan your life around scientific data. Go into your heart space and ask how you can best live each moment right now.

affirmation

I make decisions for my health. I know in my heart what is best for me.

Keep going
just a little bit more ...
just a little bit ...
just a little ...
Keep going!
Yes! Break through
that invisible barrier.
It's lighter and brighter
on the other side AND
the grass is even greener!
Just keep going ...
Keep going ...
Ahhh ...

affirmation

The rewards
are great
when I
keep going.
I keep going.
I keep going.

When your life is
put on hold due to
illness, surgery, exhaustion,
or other circumstance,
consider that time a
universal process of
rebirth where you are
being tweaked, prepared,
and tuned up for life's
next great adventure.
Use that downtime to
strengthen, regroup,
and recalibrate.
Give your human processing
the needed rest.
And know that
what is next will be
phenomenal.

affirmation

I use
this time
to rest
and heal.
My next
adventure
is grand.

Healing does not occur in stagnation. Healing requires moving from one state of being to another more beneficial state. *Healing requires change,* be it in health, emotions, feelings, or attitude.

affirmation

I welcome
the change that
healing brings.
I am ready
to clear
the way.

Illness burns out old frequency patterns and clears a path for *higher energy* to enter. It is often a recalibration of energy into a *new frequency* of light. Notice the shift in *awareness* that leads you to the *knowing* of what you are here to do. Even in illness, All Is Well.

affirmation

I clear
my mind
and let
higher energy
guide me.

When you are hit
with a sudden illness,
problems are
put on hold,
and you have the
strength and energy
to only be
in the moment.
Be gentle
with yourself and
allow your
physical body
to *heal*.

affirmation

All is
well
as I
heal now.

With healing comes a *higher perspective* and a stronger sense of self. *Welcome* a new perspective. *Be strong.* Get back to perfect health. Support those who  need healing and in return receive the support you need.

affirmation

I am
an example
of
perfect health.
May others
learn from me.

When you only
pay attention to
the bad things in life,
that's all you will see.
The good will
still happen,
just not in your view.
The Universe will
oblige you by
sending more of
what you focus on,
so switch your view and
invite goodness
into your life
and watch the Universe
SMILE with you.
It really works!

affirmation

There is
goodness
all around
me.
I smile
and let
it in.

Live in your
heart space
and stay wrapped
in Spirit.
This *positive* energy
will keep you
connected and keep
your vibration high.
When annoying
negativity wants to
drag you down,
you'll be
well protected ...
AND your light-ness
will dissipate ✹
the negative force.

affirmation

I change
my vibration
and resonate
in light.
Only goodness
and light
prevail.

The beauty of *being alive* is you get to *experience life* from different ages. So keep your vessel in top shape so that you can be here to *fully appreciate* the wisdom available with each year.

affirmation

I am wise.
I learn
from life.
My wisdom
carries on.

Take some time off from worrying. You'll discover that life still goes on ... and ... you will have *new energy* to see your situation from a *better perspective*.

affirmation

My mind
is clear.
I see
the truth.
I am
in control.

Don't let the number of your age determine your state of **HEALTH** or how you see yourself. Having a **PASSION FOR LIFE** and living it to the fullest is the **BEST WAY** to be ageless. Aging does not mean deteriorating. So challenge convention. Adopt an **AGELESS ATTITUDE** and don't let a number hold you back.

affirmation

I AM AN
AGELESS
WONDER.
I AM
HEALTHY
AND I GLOW.

When you take
a break — a vacation,
a timeout, a minute,
or a breath —
indulge in it *completely*.
You chose to take
that time for yourself,
so use it without
dragging along the
very problems from
which you need
the break.
Your time — your break.
Decision done!

affirmation

These moments
are for
me.
My time.
My break.
Ahhh ...

When you hold your breath in fear, you stop the natural flow of energy through your body. When energy backs up and pools in any particular area, different ailments can manifest. The best antidote for fear is breath. *Breathe* through your aches and pains. *Breathe* through your fear. *Breathe*, and let the energy flow.

affirmation

I breathe.
I breathe.
I breathe.

Often, a breakthrough is preceded by periods of doubt, uncertainty, and the desire to give up. This is the physical experience of an *energy shift*. It is best to *go forward* through and with this rather than retreat and repeat over and over again. The painful familiar is not the best option. *Break through* and find out what the universe has planned for you.

affirmation

The energy
moves me
forward.
I keep going.
Great things
are planned
for me.

Don't let other people's burdens hold you back. *Keep moving forward* and open the way for them to see that there is something other than what they're stuck in. Let them *follow your light* so they can move out of their tunnels. Don't be a victim of others' circumstances.

affirmation

I stay strong as I move forward. My light leads the way.

Make
your health
a priority,
not something
you fit in
only when you
have the time.
Make time
to be healthy.

affirmation

I enjoy being healthy. Good health is my priority.

Struggling is a sign that you need to look at a situation from a *different perspective* rather than continue in the same constricting way. In struggle, there is always *another way*.

affirmation

I welcome the opportunity to better my situation. I accept that there is another way.

You don't have to feel bad to feel *better*. Treat yourself to a *healthy* boost of "feel good" while you're feeling *fine*. It helps prevent the bad times from even popping in.

affirmation

I enjoy
feeling good.
I welcome
the experience
of feeling
even better.

Take a slow, deep breath and let tension, worry, and fear dissipate, rather than breathe shallow and invite them to stay. *Breathe* ... just breathe ... and open yourself to *peace* and *calm*. All it takes is a few slow, deep breaths.

affirmation

I breathe
in calm.
My slow,
gentle
breathing
brings me
peace.
I breathe.
I
breathe.

Guilt is a wasted emotion. You lament over things past in the hopes of changing what was already done so that the present can be different. Whew!
It's better to figure out time travel!
Get on with living.

affirmation

I live now ...
fully and
completely
in the
present.

*D*on't be afraid
to heal.
When ENERGY MOVES
and
CHANGES OCCUR
during the
healing process,
you will feel different.
Don't let fear of
new sensations stop
the energy from
doing its magic.
Allow the flow to
move through you.
LET HEALING HAPPEN.
Breathe!

affirmation

I invite
healing energy
to move
through me.
Perfect health
is mine.

Sometimes you have to say no for your *self-preservation*, even when it might rattle a few nerves in others. In the long run, your *peace of mind* will benefit many more than you realize at the time.

affirmation

I do
what is best
for me.
I maintain
my power
in a
loving way.

What separates the *joyful* from the miserable is *attitude*. Adopt a *good* one and watch the *blessings* come your way.

affirmation

My attitude
is
positive.
My life
is blessed
with joy.

Same you.
Different day.
Another *opportunity*
to adjust
your plan to align
with your
heart's desire.
All things
are *possible.*
Your belief
makes it so!

affirmation

New day,
new plan.
All
is
possible.

There does not always have to be something wrong. When one ailment goes away, do not replace it with something else. Learn to be healthy — physically, emotionally, and mentally.

affirmation

I accept perfect health. I revel in its sensation.

There are always moments of *peace* during a storm – precious time to catch your breath and regroup. It's those moments that let you know it is *possible* for all to be well. Be sure to recognize them because what you focus on *expands*.

affirmation

I cherish
the moments
of peace
and calm
so that more
can enter
my life.

A setback is not forever...
so take a chance
at being *alive*...
Indulge in life!
Even if you do go
one step back,
don't fret!
You already went three
steps *forward*
just by taking a
chance at *life*.

affirmation

As I
go
forward,
I let
life
happen.

Everyone can claim a specific health condition. It is your attitude toward that condition and how much power you give to it that will determine how you live your life. You are powerful. You are more than a condition.

affirmation

I am powerful. I am greater than my condition.

When you stop being afraid that you might die, you'll begin to find out why you're alive.

affirmation

◇

I am
here for
a reason
and
the reason
is good.

◇

LIVE a vibrant, productive life by tuning into your intuition and TRUSTING that your HEART knows more than your intellect wants you to believe. ♡

My heart guides me. I trust and listen to it.

When you let someone keep you on the back burner, you will always be simmering. *Step up* to the front and *be cool!*

affirmation

I speak
what's right
with love.
I am
in
control.

Embrace THE CHANGES THAT ACCOMPANY IMPROVING HEALTH, RATHER THAN FEAR SOMETHING ELSE IS WRONG. *Allow* HEALING ENERGY TO MOVE THROUGH YOU. DON'T LET THE FEAR OF NEW SENSATIONS STOP THE FLOW OF HEALING ENERGY. *Acknowledge* THE FEAR, THEN LET IT GO.

affirmation

New sensations means I'm alive! I let the energy flow!

Good things happen all the time. It's a matter of tuning into what is *positive* and *good* rather than focusing on the expected negative and bad.

affirmation

Show me
the
positive.
I focus
on
that.

When things start going your way, don't muck it up by inventing something wrong just to avoid the responsibility of being happy.

affirmation

I accept
happiness
into my
life.
Good things
come my
way.

There is always something to *appreciate*. No matter how hopeless, desperate, or disconnected you may feel, finding just one thing to *be grateful* for goes a long way in lifting your spirit. Focus on one and another will always present itself.

affirmation

I am
connected
to the
grander
purpose.
I am
grateful
for life.

Perfect timing
happens often.
You may not
always realize that
in the moment,
especially when
the outcome is
different from what
you planned.
The Universe may
have better
plans for you.
Follow the flow.

affirmation

I trust that all is divinely planned.

Self-healing
is more in tune
with your
individual vibration
and therefore
more *lasting*.
Know that you have
the *power* of
self-healing within you.
Tap into that power
and embrace
lasting *wellness*.

affirmation

Healing happens within me. My power makes it so!

When life halts you in a panic *just keep swimming.* It's best to remember that you can. Engage your water wings. Your *natural instinct* will keep your head above water and you'll notice that you are indeed breathing. *Just keep swimming!*

affirmation

My abilities
are great.
I am
alive and
I thrive.

Your uphill
climb allows
you to be
King of
the mountain.
Claim your
mountaintop —
you earned it.

affirmation

I am
strong.
My strength
brings me
to the
top.

Spontaneous HEALING occurs when one steps out of the lower vibration in which illness is born and into a HIGHER VIBRATION where illness never exists.

affirmation

SPONTANEOUS
HEALING
HAPPENS.
I CHOOSE
TO BE
THE PROOF.

Hang in there!
Even when you feel
you are all alone
in your journey,
support is
all around you and
very much *within* you.
The support may not
be readily visible;
that's why you
must *persevere*.
Your inner *strength*
will carry you through.

affirmation

I am strong.
I carry on.
Spirit gives me strength.

*W*ho *I am* is not who I will be, because there is ever constant *change*. Knowing this gives me permission to be greater  than my limitations.

affirmation

I soar!
My spirit
leads
the
way.

Change your belief of "too good to be true" to "so good and so true," then keep both shoes on so that there's nothing else to drop. Momentum follows the energy. Keep yours *positive*.

affirmation

I accept
all
goodness
that
comes
my way.

PHYSICAL MOVEMENT CHANGES STAGNANT ENERGY. WHEN YOU ARE FEELING STUCK IN ANY WAY, *Move!* BOUNCE, SWING, JUMP, WALK, DANCE! MOVEMENT REALIGNS THE ENERGY FLOW. SO ...

Get Moving!

affirmation

I activate
my energy
to flow
abundantly
for my
health and
highest good.

What is best for your health? Your body knows, even when you pretend otherwise. *Go within.* Hang out with your spirit. *Ask!* Your body won't lie. The *answers* are right there waiting to be *discovered*.

affirmation

All I
need to
know is
within me.
I ask
and
I receive.

When you are the stressed one, know that the cheerful ones may have as much stress as you and choose a *smile* anyway. Let their *good cheer* be contagious. When you are the cheerful one, keep it going. Someone else may need the *boost*!

affirmation

I surround
myself with
positive energy.
I accept it
and pass
it along.

It is possible to have internal calm even when experiencing external chaos. It requires detaching from the emotion of the external event, with a simple, conscious breath, and saying, *This, too, shall pass.*

affirmation

This, too, shall pass. This, too, shall pass.

Sometimes you have to take a break from obsessing about your state of less-than-desirable health and engage in moments of *joyful living.* What you focus on *expands.*

affirmation

Oh,
the world
and all
its joys!
I take
pleasure in
noticing
them.

Positive thoughts benefit your health. *Belief* that "all is well" makes it so. Be positive ... Let your thoughts SMILE!!!

affirmation

Yes! I am positive. I let myself smile.

Your forward journey TOWARD OPTIMAL HEALTH ALLOWS *positive* ENERGY TO BECOME YOUR *new foundation*. LOOK BACK ONLY TO SEE HOW FAR YOU'VE COME.

affirmation

I made it this far and I continue onward. Positive, Positive, Positive — SMILE!

Know THAT
AS YOU MOVE
THROUGH GRIEF,
YOU LEARN
THE STRENGTH OF
your heart.
YOUR SPIRIT
CARRIES YOU
THROUGH.

affirmation

My heart
holds my
strength.
My Spirit
carries me
through.

You are here in this life…
Might as well live it!
Wishing for something else prevents you from experiencing what is readily available now.

affirmation

I fully live
my life
and make
this
moment
MINE!

Do not give up your *good health* just to be in the spotlight. *Consistent health* is far better than persistent drama. *Choose health* and leave drama to the stage.

affirmation

I am
a model
of
good health.
I speak
in a
healthy
way.

Recognize the times when you are so immersed in the moment that you forget about your troubles. This is *validation* that it is *possible* for all to be *well*.

affirmation

I notice
the times
I am
feeling good.
I carry
this
wellness
forward.

Negative words set limits on your life. Break through negative barriers. Know that you CAN, you DO, and you ARE.

affirmation

YES!
I CAN.
I DO.
I AM!

What's right!

AT LEAST FOR TODAY, LET'S FOCUS ON KEEPING RIGHT RATHER THAN FIXING WRONG.

affirmation

In this moment, I find what is right.

Think positive.
Move forward.
Give thanks.
Have
 *wealth*
in
health ...
AMEN.

affirmation

In mind, body, and soul, optimal health is my goal!

Acknowledgments

My heartfelt gratitude to all who continue to support my journey. The overwhelming enthusiasm received on my first book Spirit Says . . . Be Inspired encouraged me to fill this sequel with extra loving energy and a desire to return the positive support during your journeys.

To my entire family, extended family and friends, I give continued smiles of gratitude.

To my etheric support team, I cherish your continued guidance.

To my earthly collaborators during this go-round, George and Jeffrey, your insight continues to be welcomed and appreciated.

A special thank you to Carol Fitzpatrick, who, through her guidance, told me I would write thirty books. I now understand the urgency to share the wisdom given to me. As I remember your words, my writing journey begins to blossom.

To Dr. Diane Barton, thank you for playing an important role in my personal healing journey.

To Stacey Aaronson, my visionary guide, you created another masterpiece as impressive as the first. Thank you for believing. And Dana . . . your quiet support is akin to cheese on a pizza!

Thank you Spirit for your ever gentle nudges that keep me in the flow.

And, again, to my husband, Jim, thank you for taking the journey with me. LUA

About the Author

author photo by Rachel

Susan Bova, PhD, is a doctor of holistic health, a visionary, a seer, and an intuitive healer. Her mission is to motivate, educate, and inspire others to achieve optimal states in mind, body, and spirit, and to fully engage their sixth-sensory intuitive sides. As an inspirational speaker, Susan combines wisdom with humor to gently encourage others to expand their horizons, welcome new perspectives, and embrace intuition. She runs a private practice in suburban Chicago.

www.drsusanbova.com

For more inspiring quotes, visit Susan's Facebook page at:
facebook.com/DrSusanBova

www.ingramcontent.com/pod-product-compliance
Lightning Source LLC
Chambersburg PA
CBHW040416100526
44588CB00022B/2842